I dedicate this book to my rainbow family.

Roland Nitzel

THEIR HEINOUS CRIME

AUSTIN MACAULEY PUBLISHERS™

LONDON • CAMBRIDGE • NEW YORK • SHARJAH

Ordering Information
Quantity sales: Special discounts are available on quantity purchases by corporations, associations, and others. For details, contact the publisher at the address below.

Publisher's Cataloging-in-Publication data
Nitzel, Roland
Their Heinous Crime

ISBN 9781685626525 (Paperback)
ISBN 9781685626532 (ePub e-book)

Library of Congress Control Number: 2023910937

www.austinmacauley.com/us

First Published 2023
Austin Macauley Publishers LLC
40 Wall Street, 33rd Floor, Suite 3302
New York, NY 10005
USA

mail-usa@austinmacauley.com
+1 (646) 5125767

A huge thank you to Margo Ellis and Eric Nitzel for their advice and enthusiastic encouragement.

Also, a very special thank you to Jaidyn Davis for her amazing cover drawing.

Their Heinous Crime

Elijah was a prophet in the Old Testament who
taught and preached faithfulness to
Yahweh.

Elijah McClain was another canary in the
coal mine. He was one of God's gentle
sweet angels who played his violin for
lonely cats and dogs

Asthmatic Elijah Mclain was walking home from
the store, listening to music, waving his arms,
wearing a ski mask.

A good citizen called the police. She said
he's weird. You better check him out

He was a five-foot, six-inch, 140-pound
massage therapist

Soon he was surrounded by policemen
and paramedics. He tried to explain who
he was and what he was doing. They wouldn't
listen; they choked him out twice!

and gave him a double shot of a powerful
sedative. A few days later, he died.

I

Emmett Till, a 14-year-old boy,
visiting his family in Mississippi was accused
of flirting with or whistling at a young
white women

Her husband and his brother
found and dragged Emmett from his
cousin's house, before shooting him
in the head, they beat and mutilated his
body and then discarded him in the
Tallahatchie River

Years later, the women said Emmett
did not deserve what her husband
and brother-in-law did to him.

Dick Rowland, a 19-year-old black
shoe shiner in a Tulsa hotel tripped
and fell as he was getting into an
elevator operated by Sarah Page
She squealed!

A concerned white desk clerk
called the police
they jailed Dick

A mob of hundreds of white men
gathered outside the jail

Rumors of a possible lynching spread
through the city

Seventy-five armed black men arrived
at the jail, ready to protect the prisoner

One of the white men tried to disarm one
of the black men. During the struggle,
the black man shot the white man,
igniting the Tulsa Race Massacre, aka
the Black Wall Street Massacre

The Greenwood neighborhood was called
Black Wall Street because it had an
extremely successful economy and
community of black people

There was a luxury hotel, grocery stores,
a library, churches, barber shops, hairdressers,
banks, and much more

A prosperous stable community

Cheered on by the local newspaper
the mob raged for 16 hours

The destruction of property and life was
horrific
For the first and last time in American
history, owners of private planes bombed
their fellow citizens

9

One hundred and fifty to 300 black
people were killed, 800 were injured,
ten thousand were homeless

Thirty-five square blocks were destroyed.
One thousand, two hundred homes were
demolished

In the end, Sarah refused to press charges
against Dick Rowland.

Elijah McClain, Emmett Till, the residents of Greenwood…
what was their heinous crime?

COVID-19

Measuring our days
with rolls of toilet paper
too much time
roaming in our heads

Wondering
Are we just cannon fodder
for politicians?

Rage against the invisible terror
rage against the unbelievers
rage against the un-leaders
who brought us to this
moment

When will it end?

My Feet Need to Dance

My feet need to dance.
but I have no rhythm

My voice needs to sing,
but my ears are tone-deaf

My eyes paint brilliant golden sunflowers, and
the red hills of Abiquiu
but my hand shakes

I have significant sermons to deliver
but my voice quakes

My mind's camera snaps photographs
of unbearable pathos
but my photos are blurred

My Racial Education

I

We,
Mommy and me,
sit in the high summer
pasture grass. I am four years
old

Our one-room house is
up the hill behind us

Behind the house is
Mt Saint Helens

Across the crick is
the big house,
my grandparent's house,
a square four-roomed
gray wood shake building

Below at the bottom
of the hill on this side of the crick,
two men are dismantling an old car,

loading the removed parts into
the back of a pickup

Mommy: "Why are they
black?"
"Shh, hush,
they have really good hearing."

II

First grade:
We are living in town now
Daddy works up river clearing
and burning brush all day
making room for the new dam

At the end of the day,
he comes home to our ex-motel a
two room cabin, with a pint

His skin is completely covered
with black soot

He pours some of the
whiskey into an empty jelly jar,
goes into the bathroom to
wash off the soot
A noisy car enters
our dark compound.
a car door is opened and shut.

there's a tentative knock on our door

Mother opens the door
I half hide behind her
a black woman is standing
in the doorway

"Hello, ma'am, I'm Esther
That short one over there is my
husband Floyd and that real
black one is my brother, LeRoy
we are new around here
Do you know where folks
like us can stay?"

III

Sixth grade:
Laramie Wyoming
Billy Boy and I are walking
home from school, walking west
toward the railroad tracks

Our assignment for the weekend
is to write about our ancestors and
where they are from

I announce that mine are from
Europe and yours are from
Africa

He protests,
"No, we're not. We're from
Alabama!"

I start to explain
He cuts me off

"I ain't from any damned Africa!"

IV

Junior High,
waiting in the auditorium

The administration has
invited a traveling Minstrel show,
adult white men in black makeup,
to edify and entertain us

The show starts,
comic skits, jokes, dancing, singing
general merriment

Minstrel shows portray black people as
lazy, dim-witted, and superstitious

A Minstrel show depicts black people as
happy-go-lucky slaves in good old
'bama.

Billy Boy didn't smile, he didn't laugh,
he didn't clap

A Minstrel show is
designed to crush the spirit of a
young black boy and the soul
of all black people.

City Championship

On Championship Day, Billy Boy and I walked to the gym

Five years, we walked to Saturday matinees,
to the river to skinny-dip, to the Salvation Army to
play basketball

We were caught stealing returnable Coke bottles
from the neighborhood whore house

Five years, we walked
played all-day Sunday football games
in city park, played at love with the
neighborhood girls in night-filled,
garbage-filled alleys.

On Championship Day, Billy Boy and I walked to the
gym.

We dressed in the quiet nervous locker room and entered
the gym crowded with contestants, referees, new white
plastic mats, and one lone devoted suburban mother
ready for Championship Day.

Whistles blew, muscles erupted, bodies twisted, circled, spun, vied for position. Sweat, pain, exhilaration, defeat, elation, and exhaustion permeated the room

And one devoted suburban mother cheered only for her son. He won his division.

Our weight competition began
match after match we both won, our names crawled across the scorekeeper's sheet until they met

One of us would be the champion

The whistle blew, and our white and black bodies collided in the middle of the mat, skin burning on plastic

Suddenly one devoted suburban honkey mother screamed wildly, "Don't let that 'boy' beat you."

The whistle blew. Billy Boy took the blue, I the red

I was ecstatic, I knew we were the best
Billy Boy threw his arms around me
clutching his blue ribbon
tears racing down his
ebony cheeks

Porcelain Buddha

A few familiar mementos rest
on an orange crate bookshelf

A picture of an autumn scene I had
cut out of a magazine and framed
hangs on the wall

From the bookshelf,
a smooth milk white
magic fertility Buddha
scrutinizes me

A gift from Peter the
proprietor of our favorite
Chinese restaurant

He told us to rub its
belly and wish for a
boy or girl

So, long ago, I rubbed his
slick white magic belly and
made a wish. Her name is Renee.

He continues staring at me
exploring my soul,reviewing
the sins of my youth
if I rub his belly, will he
grant me forgiveness?

Cowboys and Indians

Bang! Bang! Gotcha. You're
dead

His stick gun snapping with
tremendous recoil
Wild Bill Jesse James Billy
Kid, dives behind a garbage
can spews Budweiser cans half-
eaten tortillas, and a Wheaties
box across the alley and takes
deadly aim

Missed me!
Bang! Bang! Bang!

Bullets blazing
Crazy Horse Geronimo Sitting Bull
deftly scales Mr. Wilson's stockade fence

Through dirt alleys and grass-bare yards
over tin-roofed sheds under a jacked-up Studebaker
around the whorehouse until Maggie,
the madman, scares them off

White Deer and Kit Carson chase each other down the
dusty alley

At lunch time, the battle nears Sundance's
basement apartment

He runs around the corner,
opens the door, runs down
the concrete steps into
the living room, removes
his older brother's 30.06
from the gun rack

Screaming, Cochise thunders
down the steps, leaps into the
room

Sundance makes his
last stand.

Bang! Gotcha.

On a Dusty Road

Walking in the middle of the
road to Damascus, I wait
for the blinding light

Autos whirl by honking
tires, throwing dust into
my face

I am quite comfortable here
I have waited before

I have backpacked up the
Rocky Mountains, searching for
a burning bush
and I waited

I have pilgrimage to Israel looking
for a strange longing, for a
strange warming of the heart
and I waited

I have worn camel's hair
and eaten grasshoppers dipped
in wild honey
and I waited

I have wandered through the
Sonora Desert, peyote, and Arizona
sun-fried my brain
and I waited

I have attended finely
orchestrated revivals, fallen
to my knees, weeping in
harmony with Amazing Grace
just as I am

I wait
I wait
I wait

The Sixties

Thousands rushing back and forth
like Lemmings, running from the Atlantic to
the Pacific and back, across the dessert, over the
Rocky Mountains, across prairies and farmlands, over the
Alleghenies, to the Atlantic, and back again, running faster,
to get there, to get away from there, to find it,
to lose it

Thousands of teenagers, college students, university
professors, clerk typists, computer programmers,
housewives, draft-dodgers, deserters, dropouts, drop-ins,
all running faster and faster, Jack Kerouac, Neal Cassady,
Allen Ginsberg Ken Kesey, and Timothy Leary are their
prophets, running across America running, searching,
fleeing, faster, faster, faster.

Hundreds and thousands, hundreds of thousands,
millions speeding from coast to coast, from crash pads
in the Village, to Oregon communes, from San Francisco,
to Wounded Knee, from Chicago ghetto to Big Sur,
from acid, to Annie Greensleeves, from Zen to Jesus freak,
from peyote to health food, from bed to bed.

Night Visit

On an ancient clipper,
I visited a strange new land,
yet a world I had visited
many times.

A land of Indian Ocean sun
a land of painful clarity
a land of mystery and
ambiguity

Wading in the breakers,
she met me

We walked and talked on
the white beach, her
slender toes imprinted
for a moment in the sand
forever in my eyes.

Her villa was perched high
on the rugged cliff

When she entered the
building, the doorway
shrunk until it disappeared.

I could not enter chambers
once easily accessible
chambers of peace and torment
known places, and sanctuaries
lost

Don't you Dare

Don't tell me your black and brown
lies
Don't send me your black and brown
jokes
Don't whisper your snide remarks in my
ear
Don't expect me to share your evil
poison
I will not wallow with you
in your cesspool of hate

A Perfect Day

Yellow and red leaves
dance to the tunes
the wind plays

The clear sky is
warm

From the park
across the street,
the loud thump of a
perfectly struck
soccer ball

Crowd cheers

A perfect shot,
a perfect goal,
a perfect day!

Two Gentlemen

Friday night, Mom said, "Why don't
you go out to the old quarry tomorrow
afternoon and get us two or three
cottontails, and I'll make hasenpfeffer
for Sunday supper?

This week, they gave me my
first gun, a present for my
twelfth birthday
It is a single shot 22, last winter.
I learned to shoot at the Laramie
police department.

I'm a member of the Police Activities
League, they also taught us gun
safety.

Saturday, after lunch, Dad drove
me out to the quarry
and dropped me off

My hunting ground isn't in the
quarry. It is in the sagebrush
above the quarry. I circle up
and around the rim and start
hunting

It didn't take much time to
bag three rabbits

Dad said he would pick me up at
about 3 o'clock. I don't have a
watch, so I found a comfortable rock
on the edge of the rim

I wait and watch two red tailed hawks
gliding high above the prairie
The wind is picking up, dust starts blowing,
trying to become a dust devil

After a while, I see a car pull off
the highway. I watch its dust
trail as it drives toward me

It isn't our car

Below me, the car stops in the middle
of the quarry. Two young guys, maybe
from the university, get out of the car

They face each other and
start hitting each other hard

I can hear the loud smacks
as fists hit faces

I have seen and participated in
school yard fights. This one
is eerily quiet

The fight ends. I don't
know who won

They shake hands,
get into the car, and
drive away.

About ten minutes later,
Dad came and drove me
and the rabbits home

Sunday Afternoon

Heavy raindrops pound the old
red and white Chevy pickup
parked in the dirt yard. Minute
atomic mushroom clouds dance
in the mud puddles

Sitting on the couch reading
the paperback edition of
Catcher in The Rye, the one
with Holden facing away from the reader
wearing a red cap backwards on his
head and a red scarf
around his neck

Holden calls it a hunting hat,
must be an eastern thing

Grandpa and Grandma have
fallen asleep in their chairs
flexes of tobacco surround both chairs
Grandpa rolls his cigarettes by hand
Grandma has a little machine she uses
A western novel rests on Grandpa's chest

Grandma's solitaire cards are on her footstool

It is raining much harder now. The
mushroom clouds are getting larger

I don't know if I like this Holden guy
I like the way he tells the story, but
all he does is complain and judge
He even complains about people
talking about gas mileage
I think he is a snob

The rain is letting up

I do like the way he's telling
his story

I guess I'll give him a break and
finish reading his book

The Fiddler

As the un-leader fiddles with twitter,
two thousand a day
die

He cares for your parents and grandparents,
very little

As he fiddles with his scorecard,
three thousand a day
die

He cares for your friends and neighbors,
very little

As the other un-leaders fiddle with their
diddles
hiding from the un-leader,
four thousand a day
die

They care for you and your children and grandchildren,
very little

The Ranch

'Oh, me, oh, oh my, oh Jambalaya,' sings
another aspiring coal miner's daughter

Tuesday night, Dionysian Disciples
prance around the packed dance floor
swaying and twisting to
hybrid disco-square dance.

Orange county secretaries, programmers,
West Texas transplants, and out-of-town
insurance men, all converted
to instant stompers

The self-proclaimed
best damned redneck band
in Southern California plays
country, bluegrass, old rock,
Johnny Cash,
Chuck Berry,
Hank Williams,
Willie Nelson

Paraplegic young men in wheelchairs
dance with saintly sensuous nymphs
their chairs float across the floor in
perfect synch with the music

A melancholy young man
with a black patch over his left eye
broods over his drink while
Marian the Librarian
presses against a drunk cowboy

The worshippers hoot and howl
when a bevy of maidens
perform the ritual of the
wet t-shirt contest

Some measure their lives
with coffee spoons,
others chug mugs
of cold beer

Saved

Saved
from what?

Saved
from a medieval hell,
eternally wandering in Dante's Inferno or
locked in a Hieronymus Bosch painting
forever tormented by
the flames of Hades

Saved
from guilt
sins of the flesh
sins of the world

Saved
from the devil
which is me

Saved
from pride

Saved
from questions, skepticism, cynicism

Saved
from death

Nothing before
Nothing after

Kenosha

An under-aged interloper, a devotee of hate
an acolyte of the un-leader, struts up
and down dark curfewed streets
brandishing an assault weapon

His mommy drove him there
from another state.

A young black man, Jacob Blake
father of three young children
lies paralyzed and shackled
to a hospital bed.

The authorities give the interloper
water, food, and praise.

The young black man is in pain and
confused.

His children watched and listened
as a policeman at point blank
pumped seven bullets
into their father's back

The under-aged vigilante
patrols the dark streets
looking for targets
wounds one
kills two

The authorities praise him
They blamed the protesters for
breaking curfew

The un-leader defends
him

His mommy drives him
back to their state

The young black man wonders,
Will I walk again?
Will I love again?
Will I die?

I'm Late

I'm late for a very, very
important date with
my mate, concerning
selling bait, on
roller-skates

I Don't Get Why You
Don't Get It

Black lives matter
Black lives matter too

Are you deliberately so obtuse
that you can't admit that for
four centuries, American black
people have been told and shown
they don't matter

They have been enslaved, beaten,
bought and sold like cattle, whipped,
told they are a different kind
that they have a weaker mind

Without a trial, they have been
lynched by the thousands

In modern times, they have been
under-educated and over-imprisoned
They have been redlined
and left behind
You think it is clever to point out

that white lives matter, that
blue lives matter, that all lives matter.
You should be clever enough to know
we already know.

What ever happened to walking
a mile in the other guy's shoes?
What ever happened to the
Golden Rule?

Black lives matter too!

Blessed or Damned

What shall we say then? Is there unrighteousness with God?

God forbid!

The doorbell buzzes
Our five-day-old daughter
whimpers in her sleep. I
rush to the door. Mother
and child need to rest

A nondescript man in a brown suit stands under
the yellow-white porch light

"'O man', who art thou to ask such questions of Him?"

"Come in, I'd like to talk with you about this matter." He
enters the room. I offer him the couch.
He chooses a straight-backed kitchen chair.

I begin, "Well sir, I would like to know
who is saved and who isn't. Is it predestination
or random or are we judged by our deeds?"

"My son, remember what He said to Moses.
I will have mercy on whom I will have mercy, and
I will have compassion on whom
I will have compassion."

"Okay, okay, I know it's impossible
for Him to not know the final score, but damn!
Why does He have to fix the game?"

"Calm down, my son,
hath not the potter power over
the clay, of the same lump to make
one vessel unto honor and another
unto dishonor?"

"Oh, man! That's beautiful! Think
of this, sir, would a good potter deliberately
misuse his clay? He wouldn't, and if
he made a mistake he would destroy the ruined
vessel and start over."

The visitor rose from the stiff chair
and walked to the door, opened it,
and quietly left

What shall we say then? Is there unrighteousness with God?

God forbid!

Hayduke Lives

This morning, Santa Fe,
tonight Needles

Billboards and dead jackrabbits
tourist gift shops, come on in and
see the two-headed rattlesnake,
black lava beds and graceful
soaring turkey buzzards

Stuckey's and pinyon forests,
pink sandstone swirls and power
plants, magpies, and diesel exhaust

Red bluffs and juniper trees
oil refineries and Navajo shepherds,
hogans and abandoned cars
snow-capped mountains
and highway litter

Albuquerque, Gallup, Holbrook, Winslow
Flagstaff, Kingman, Needles.

I kneel on the banks of the Colorado
while behind me on the highway,
thousands of later-day Joads rush west
to the promised land and I
pray for the return of the
Monkey WrenchGang.

Raise up, ye men and women of Window Rock.
Raise up, ye men and women of Green River.
Raise up, ye men and women of Boulder.
Raise up, ye men and women of Hoboken.
Raise up and save us from the power plants,
the oil refineries, the billboards, the litter,
and the junk cars

Hayduke lives!

Amen

The Riot

I didn't go back to the farm
this year.

Mandatory summer school, I
barely passed seventh-grade
math

In class, I pretended I was reading
my math book, but I was really
reading novels hidden inside
my textbook

Tonight is the last night of *Laramie
Jubilee Days*

When the carnival came to town
I got a job working in a booth
where people throw darts at
balloons

We just finished taking down
the booth and loading it and
other booths and equipment
onto trucks

As they drive away
a band starts setting up on
a wooden stage at the corner
of Third Street and Grand Avenue
the main intersection in town

A crowd is quickly gathering around the musicians.
It is a mixed crowd, students from the
university, some kids from the
high school, and lots of people
wearing cowboy hats; blue jeans,
and boots.

The music starts, and the
dancing starts, and the
drinking starts.

I watch them dancing and drinking beer

When a non-dancer puts their
beer bottle on a store windowsill
and joins the dancers, I pick up the
bottle and have a swig

The crowd continues to grow
I continue my search for
abandoned beer bottles
everyone is having a
merry time

A car horn starts rapidly honking
it is trying to push through the
intersection

The crowd instantly becomes a mob
They surround the car and pound
on the hood. A couple of guys jump
on the bumpers and start bouncing
the car

A young boy and girl are in the backseat
their faces squashed against the window,
their terrified eyes pleading for help

Eventually, the mob releases the
car. As it drives away, I see the
out-of-state license plate

I stagger into the ally and throw up

You are Not

If you label a captured
war hero a loser,
you are not a
patriot

If you ridicule mothers and fathers
who lost sons and daughters in
the never-ending war
you are not a
patriot

If you brag about sexually assaulting women
by grabbing their private parts,
you are not a role
model

If you mock a handicapped person
on national television,
you are not a role
model

If you are a parent, a grandparent, a youth leader, and you
aren't horrified by this behavior,
you are not a role
model

If you put your knee on our throats
trying to stop us from voting,
you are not a defender of
democracy

If you are a co-conspirator,
you are not a defender of
democracy

My Rainbow Family

I celebrate my rainbow family:
black, white, brown, Northern Europeans,
Latinos, Navajo, Choctaw, Jewish, gay, lesbian,
straight, Presbyterians, Later-day Saints, agnostics

It is easy and lazy to stereotype us
that doesn't even come close
to knowing us

First and foremost, we are human beings

We bleed the same as you
We feel pain the same as you
We need love the same as you
We want respect the same as you
We want to be judged as individuals
the same as you

Saturday Night Dance

I am six years old.
we are still living in town.
most Saturday afternoons,
we come back to the farm
in the valley, and we stay
until after Sunday supper.

We do chores, mending fences,
chopping wood, haying, and milking;
there are always chores

Saturday nights are dance nights
at the schoolhouse that is no longer
a schoolhouse

Because it has a gym, and a kitchen,
and a big room for the potluck meal
halfway through the night, it is
the perfect place for a
Saturday-night dance

I'm waiting for Mommy and Daddy
in the grassless yard. I want to get there
so I can play with the other kids.

Finally, they come out of the house.
We start walking. Grandpa and Grandma
will drive down when they are done watching
the Lawrence Welk Show

Some kids are already there. We
run around yelling and screaming,
playing hide-and-seek
and kick-the-can

More and more cars are coming
down the gravel road
They are coming from farms
on the other side of the hill
and many are from our town
and some from other towns.

Soon we can hear the caller
inside the building

Bow to your partner.
Bow to your corner.
Circle left. Circle right.
Do-si-do and allemande left
and allemande right
forward and back and
promenade home.

We play outside until it's
time to eat.

Tables in the big room are
loaded with fried chicken, baked beans
potato salad, Waldorf salad, three-bean
salad, every kind of casserole you
can think of, cakes and pies,
cookies and homemade ice cream.

After the meal, the music starts again
A man and a young boy are playing accordions

They play waltzes and polkas. Grandpa
and Grandma always leave after
they play the Tennessee Waltz

More square dancing and
accordion playing

Mommy announces it's time
to leave.

The music slowly fades behind us
as we walk up the dark road
Daddy lifts me up onto his shoulders
gravel crunches under his feet
foghorns blow from the big ships

going up and down the big river
to and from Portland, the lonely
sound floats over the foothills
of Mt Saint Helens

My head slowly bends
lies on Daddy's head
I am wondering what kind
of pie Grandma is going to
make for Sunday's dinner
dessert: apple, cherry, blackberry,
maybe lemon merin ...

I Like and Respect

I like and respect the policeman who
stopped in a snowstorm and
helped an elderly Asian lady
change a flat tire

I am thankful for the policeman
who snatched me off the streets of
Laramie and made me join the
Police ActivitiesLeague.

They taught me judo, gun
safety, wrestling, and they let
me march in the Fourth of July
parade, pretending to play
a bugle.

I don't like or respect a
shirttail relative, who was sent
to prison with 40 other officers
know in Denver as 'the burglars in blue.'

I don't like or respect the policemen
of Hilton Head Island who stopped a
black plumber six times
in one year as he was going
from one job to the next.
They called him, boy, no
tickets, no arrests, no respect
a 46-year-old man and
they called him
boy!

I don't like or respect policemen who
appoint themselves as judge, jury
and executioner.

I don't like or respect policemen who
shoot people in the back.

I don't like or respect policemen who
brag, demean, and joke about someone
they just killed

I don't like and respect policemen
who won't cross the thin blue
line and tell the truth

I like and respect the policemen who
risk their lives when they rush into
an active shooting situation

I like and respect the policeman who
said he tries to treat everyone as if
they are one of his neighbors

Denver Dance

Tap, tap, tap, click, click, heel tap, toe tap.

his blue eyes trapped
by flying rhythmic black feet

Heel toe, heel toe, tap, click
click, click, tap

White boy face,illuminated periodically by
flashing neon Coors sign, enthralled with
supple black grace

Tap, tap!

"Come on, baby! Daddy needs a ten!"
Junior Garcia, first day home from the pen
squats in the middle of a circle of Pachucos
clustered in front of the steps of an apartment building
baggy blue jeans reveal the apex of
the cleft of his fat rump, throws the
dice against the bottom step
"Snake eyes!"

Click, click!

Me and My Shadow floats from the jukebox
in the corner of the White Horse Bar and Grill
air permeated with smoke, beer, whiskey,
sweat, refritos and chile verde

Disembodied feet caress the hardwood floor

Tap, tap!

Father O'Malley pats each of the five beautiful
Morales sisters on the head as they exit St. Elizabeth's
dressed in their Sunday best, that afternoon the boy
meets Dora Morales in the alley behind her house
and trades cold white mushy slices of Wonder Bread
for warm homemade flour tortillas

Tap, click, tap, click!

A new record drops onto the turntable
black body whirls around the room
leaps onto the blue-eyed boy's table

Tap, tap, click, click, tap!

Feet sing as
they glide over the Formica tabletop.

Click, tap, click, tap!

Cool spring night, Yolanda Ulibarri
leads him into Mr. Stein's backyard
where she instructs him behind
the fragrant lilac bushes.

Heel toe, heel toe!

Gusts of autumn wind blow dry
leaves across the pavement, handsome
brown-skinned boys with liquid-brown eyes
play football on Eleventh Street in front
of the red brick firehouse, the dead yellow leaves
crackle under their running feet. They run out for
passes until they can't see the ball spiraling through the
brittle twilight air

Tap, tap, tap, click, click, tap!

Nancy Silver Nails, crazy drunk leans out of her
second-floor apartment window and waves at
the paper boy, inviting him to come up
He throws the paper onto the porch
and races to the next building

Click, click, tap, tap!

The black man spins, jumps, whirls, leaps,
around the room.

Rivulets of sweat course down his face.
He finishes with a grand flourish and
promenades around the saloon, smiling
benevolently as the white men toss
dimes and quarters into a battered
brown hat he holds out to them. The
boy's father drops a dollar into the hat.
the black man bows and backs
out of the bar

The Kindness of a Stranger

It was our summer of discontent. My job
was to keep our six-year-old grandson
out of the crossfire.

He and I spent endless hours at the local Jungle Gym,
an indoor trampoline establishment. It's like a
super-enormous, bouncy house with rules.
There was a section for older kids and adults,
and a kid's section, which was much smaller.

We were there night and day, almost every day.
He became very proficient at doing forward,
and backward flips. He was so good that some
of the employees nicknamed him 'flipper.'

Since he was under ten years old,
he was supposed to stay in the
little kid's section, but some quiet
afternoons when the boss wasn't

around, the teenaged employees
would let him onto the big kid's
section where he could really
show his stuff.

One night when the gym was full and we
were the only ones using the kid's section,
an older man with a boy who had
down syndrome joined us.

The other boy just ran around and
jumped up and down, and Tyler
waited for space to do a few flips.
Both boys were having a good time.
The man commented on Tyler's skill,
Other than that, we just watched.

Tyler was doing backflips and something
went wrong. He fell awkwardly and put
his hand on his neck. I could see the
fear in his eyes.

I was terrified. What if it was serious?
We had had enough turmoil that summer.

As I started to go to the desk and
ask for help, the other man said,
"Wait a minute."

He kneeled next to Tyler, bent over,
put his hand on Tyler's neck, and
started talking to him.

I don't know what the man said, but
Tyler stopped crying. The man felt
his neck again and asked him some more
questions. Tyler sat up. The man asked him
another question. Tyler stood up.

The man said, "He's okay.
He was just scared."

I asked, "Are you a doctor?
You were so calm."

He said, "I'm not a doctor. I was
an elementary school principal
for 35 years."

The boys went back to jumping and flipping.
The man and I talked.

He told me that the boy was his grandson
who was from out of state, and the whole family
was in town because his wife of 43 years
died last week and her funeral was
the next day

Running out of Time

Eleven o'clock in the morning, a wizened
apartment house manger stumbles down
the alley to The Pink Elephant bar on East Colfax.

A smoker's cough tears through his body.
His malignant black lungs expel an ugly hunk of
phlegm. He spits the wad behind a dumpster.

He is the tavern's initial patron of the day,
taking his post at the bar, he orders
a draft of beer and a shot of whiskey.

Five-thirty in the afternoon, his son finds him
still manning his station. The bar is almost full.
The boy sits down next to the old man.

His father puts his arm around his shoulders
and loudly announces to the room, "Hey, this is
my son, the honor-roll student."

Flames of shame, guilt, anger, and self-pity flare
through the boy's gut.
He slipped off the stool, letting his father's
arm thump onto the bar, and walked back
up the alley to their one-bedroom
basement apartment.

Father

Yellow-skinned leaf tugged
from its niche by autumn wind
yellow-skinned leaf scraping
across cold pavement deposited
in an obscure
gutter

Yellow-skinned father lying
in sterile whiteness of
Denver General Hospital
fighting for his life, his lungs
blackened, his liver shriveled

Yellow-skinned father torn
from his tenuous hold on life,
his ashes scattered in an obscure
gutter

Printed in the USA
CPSIA information can be obtained
at www.ICGtesting.com
LVHW091605280723
753396LV00018B/1248

9 781685 626525